NOTES

Black And Blue Lives: How to Survive and Reform American Criminal Justice

By Curtis Elmore, JD

Published By Elmore Entertainment
Copyright 2016

Vol. 11

BFBACA

2 4 5 6 8

Available on Create Space and Amazon

p. cme.

[M] 60500483

Disclaimer

The following information is not intended to be, nor should it be construed as legal advice in your state, and though what is contained herein may refer to federal constitutional law, every state has its own criminal laws and procedure. If you're in legal trouble, please consult an attorney in your state for legal advice forthwith. What is presented herein is for educational and entertainment purposes only.

Introduction

This book is the product of fifteen years of criminal
defense work in the criminal justice system in Florida. Part
I reveals some harsh truths about the system with real life
anecdotes about regular people dealing with the actual
system. Part II offers some specific suggestions as to how
people can act to avoid getting dragged into the system,
and Part III offers some specific suggestions as to how the
system should be reformed in order to advance our culture
in terms of its justice, and to bring our society into the the
21st Century.

Table of Contents

Part II: How To Survive The Criminal Justice System

Part III: Eleven measures to reform the criminal justice system.

Appendix:

PART I - Why You Have To Fight For Your Life

Ch. 1. Repent And You'll Be Crushed To The Fullest Extent Of The Law

Cut this warning right out of this book right now and put it in your wallet, or take a photo of it with your phone so that you always have it with you, and message it to all of your friends.

MIRANDA WARNING

1. YOU HAVE THE RIGHT TO REMAIN SILENT.

2. ANYTHING YOU SAY CAN AND WILL BE USED AGAINST YOU IN A COURT OF LAW.

3. YOU HAVE THE RIGHT TO TALK TO A LAWYER AND HAVE HIM PRESENT WITH YOU WHILE YOU ARE BEING QUESTIONED.

4. IF YOU CANNOT AFFORD TO HIRE A LAWYER, ONE WILL BE APPOINTED TO REPRESENT YOU BEFORE ANY QUESTIONING IF YOU WISH.

5. YOU CAN DECIDE AT ANY TIME TO EXERCISE THESE RIGHTS AND NOT ANSWER ANY QUESTIONS OR MAKE ANY STATEMENTS.

WAIVER

DO YOU UNDERSTAND EACH OF THESE RIGHTS I HAVE EXPLAINED TO YOU?
HAVING THESE RIGHTS IN MIND, DO YOU WISH TO TALK TO US NOW?

The law treats the repentant harshly.

"Everything you say can and will be used against you." You've heard it a million times, but please believe it. Just cross out the "can and" part of that statement in your mind now, so that it reads just "Everything you say will be used against you." or maybe "Open your mouth to increase your sentence."

Prosecutors love easy targets. To the prosecutor, a confession is the grandest prize, the firmest confirmation of a guilty suspect, a recognized flouting of the law, and deserving of the harshest punishment.

Defendant: *"Five years? That's the max. Man, I can't do five years. I just got out."*
Me: *"I know, but they've got you red handed because you confessed. There's no practical way to fight it at this point. You're at the mercy of the prosecutor."*
Prosecutor walks up: *"I'm sorry. I know I said five years, but I wasn't considering the statutes together correctly. It's ten years."*

When I was working for the public defender in Miami, I met this young kid who was twenty-two years old. He was a punk, no doubt, but he was young and naïve, with little or no parental supervision, bad friends, and an even worse life-path.

He had just been released from prison where he had done a three-year stint for his part in a burglary, and now he was back in jail for another burglary. This time he had broken into someone's condo to steal anything of value, and it was telling that while he was there he stole food out of the refrigerator. The kid basically had no idea how to take care of himself, nor how to make a living, so he was living as a thief.

When he got caught this time he was very repentant. He genuinely felt bad about the harm that he caused, as revealed in his detailed, written confession.

Now you might think that when someone comes to you and confesses that you might take it a little bit easier on them than if they were unrepentant; and you may figure that the laws of the state, being a reflection of our general culture, might also afford a modicum of mercy to those citizens and in those situations wherein it's clear that the guilty party is making some effort to atone for their sins; However, that is never the case.

Every single time I was confronted with a case wherein my defendant had confessed, I was dismayed, disgruntled and discouraged to find that without exception the state prosecutors simply saw each confession as a means to exact the maximum penalty upon the defendant.

As opposed to showing mercy and being more lenient upon the repentant, the states attorneys are merciless towards confessors, seek the harshest penalties therefore, and certainly engender the highest level of resentment in the newly reformed, who I'm sure spread the word to anyone thinking of confessing.

NEVER CONFESS, it's akin to stipulating to the maximum penalty. Keep your big pie-hole shut!

The abject lesson to be learned here is that it's critical that you seek and obtain legal consultation immediately upon your recognition that you are under suspicion of anything by any agency.

Every episode of Law and Order could have been avoided if those defendants had invoked their rights to a lawyer before answering Any questions other than providing their identity.

If you're ever in a situation where you're confronted with law enforcement, the urge to tell them something, anything in the hopes that it will help will be incredibly powerful, almost overwhelming, but don't do it.

Shut the Hell up.

Ch. 2. The Poor And Minorities Get Trolled, Trapped And Trounced

Driving While Black?

I once defended a black man who had been pulled over because he did not look at the cop who pulled up next to him. The officer rolled up to the light, looked at my guy, my guy didn't look back, and that was it, and the stop was upheld by the trial judge as one in which reasonable suspicion had arisen. The officer testified that he had once read in a cop magazine that such behavior, not saying "hi" back, was suspicious. The defendant testified he never looks at cops.

While it's impossible to tell whether or not the suspicion arose due to the skin color of my client, it's important to note that the officer was driving around in low income neighborhoods when he decided to engage my client. That is the norm. That is to say, there may not be a deliberately race motivated reason for many stops, but minorities are more likely to be low income people and therefore to live in high crime areas.

Many people believe that we have a race problem in America, and maybe we do in some places, as all localities are distinct, but, where I'm from, although it manifests in a way that predominantly affects minorities, it's really a class problem. Just because a policy has a disproportionate effect on a particular race does not mean that the policy is racist, because if you think about it, every policy has a disproportionate effect on every race.

The impetus for the acts is not racism, but rather could be called classism. The rich enjoy police protection, the ability to bond out, and readily available consultation, while the poor neighborhoods are combed for violators.

Bail is available to everyone who can afford it. Of course, if you're poor, you can't afford it. So, the net effect of requiring bail is to detain all the poor people and let the rich stay out of jail, even with identical offenses.

Holding people awaiting trial on minor offenses creates a massive detrimental cycle of conviction and increased sentencing, because it becomes prudent at some point to take a plea deal for the time you've already served and get out, even if it means adding a conviction to your record. Thus the poor can count on increased records just as a matter of convenience.

The poor get further whacked if and when they're given probation. If the fees are not waived, the monthly expenses associated with probation and classes and tests can be a substantial part of the budget, even all of it. Many times I've witnessed people violate their probation by not attending a class that they could no longer afford. Back to jail they go, and back to the Judge to try to get some relief.

By now, if you're young and black, if you're reading this, you've had "The Talk" about how dangerous it is for young black men out in society today. Take heed of the warning. I have given the talk to hundreds of young black men. Today, everyone should be given the talk. Here's one version.

The Talk

"Watch out, your ass is on the line. Every time you go outside, you have to consider yourself a target of law enforcement. Consider yourself like a piece of bloody meat in an ocean full of sharks. They Are out to get you. Not you specifically, because you haven't done anything, but anyone who comes across their radar, and as a young black man you make the radar light up like a Christmas tree.

Cops are most concerned with what you're doing, so be doing something you can talk about. If you're not doing something innocent, then they'll assume you're doing something criminal, and you may get taken down, hard. If you have a job to get to, or school, and you're dressed nicely, keep a current ID handy, and present yourself well. That goes a long way towards alleviating the fears that law enforcement has of you, but, usually by the time you're interacting with the officers, it's too late. You can get shot in less than two seconds as the little boy in the Philly park with a toy gun was.

Be aware of your surroundings both in terms of environment and company, either of which can paint you as a target. When you're outside in the presence of police, do not do anything suspicious, or make any sudden movements, because that will be construed as threatening. That means don't put your hands in your pockets, or under the seat, or anywhere. Keep your hands where cops can see them, and don't hold any shiny objects in your hands when you're around police. Seriously, drop anything in your hand that reflects light whenever you're around cops.

If they tell you to freeze, FREEZE. You can speak slowly and softly if you have something very important that you must tell the officers. Otherwise, wait for their instructions.

Finally, don't be around cops. Avoid them like zombies - don't let them get close to you. Move away, stay away, slowly, discretely, but move your ass away."

Knock Knock Knock Knock

I looked through the peephole of my Miami Beach condo and saw two uniformed officers. In my second year of law school I was still very much in the mind to assist law enforcement at every turn, so I opened the door. *"Yes Sir, How can I help you?"* I said. The officer didn't say anything, he just held up a photograph of a tall, white, blond, German-looking man. In 1997, in Miami Beach, Florida, where I went to law school, as a tall, white, blond, German looking man, I suddenly realized I was a distinct minority. The photo looked very much like me, and there were very few other people around that area who would have fit that description. Fortunately for me, I knew the guy they were looking for. Luckily, I had seen him causing a ruckus at the other end of the hall just a week before. I said to the officers *"That's not me. And I know who it is. I think he has friends at the end of the hall."* For some reason they listened to me, and they went down to check that other condo, and the guy was there and they got him, but for a few seconds I was thoroughly convinced that they were going to take me into custody for the sole reason that I looked just like the guy they were after, and I couldn't have blamed them one bit if they had.

Like it or not humans profile other humans. There's no real way around it. There's no faster way for people to rapidly evaluate one another than by appearance. So wherever there's a community wherein any group that is identifiable by look commits a greater percentage of the crime than their percentage of the population would suggest, those groups will be the focus of law enforcement and perpetuate the situation until there is a statistical change in the perpetrators of crime. If you look like other perps, and, if you're black, then in many urban centers, especially in the South, you do, unfortunately, you'll have to deal with that until those statistics change.

It's not racist for the police to investigate primarily in the populations where most crimes occur, because time is of the essence in law enforcement, so to do otherwise could constitute negligence.

The tragedy of our current criminal justice system is that we arrest and incarcerate everyday people for doing everyday things that shouldn't be illegal: crimes without criminal intent, and acts without victims. This puts average citizens at odds with law enforcement.

Sadly, if you don't go to war, probably the most dangerous thing you will ever do in your life is interact with the police.

Watch the F#$& Out!

Ch. 3. Kids And The Elderly Can Commit Serious Felonies Without Even Trying

Whenever I go out to dinner I see lots of people who may never make it home that night, and instead may spend the next several years in prison. They don't know it, they don't even suspect that's a realistic possibility, but it is. I see Grandparents drinking wine with dinner, and teens exchanging glances, and I pray they don't get dragged into the system. Here are two ways that can happen.

Grandma has a glass of wine at dinner before driving home. One the way, a dog runs out in front of the car, she's in an accident and someone in her own car dies. Grandma is forcibly tested for alcohol, and fails the test. She's arrested and jailed, and bond is set at a hundred thousand dollars. The offer from the state attorney is five years prison. Grandma cannot take the stress of a trial which if she lost could mean incarceration for the remainder of her life, so she makes a deal and spends the next three years in prison.

You may find this all perfectly acceptable, but I do not. I don't believe we should imprison people for accidents, the primary reason being that where there is no bad intent, there is no culpable behavior for them to rehabilitate. Grandma was doing everything in her power to not have an accident when the accident happened. No amount of punishment can make her a better driver. No amount of punishment can equal what she feels for the loss of her family, but that apparently is no consolation to the prosecutor, who only sees a dangerous felon instead of grandma. I've seen grandparents go to prison for the results of accidents that resulted in the death of their own family members in their own car.

The two teens may sneak off to go make out. Kissing is still legal even for kids, but any touching of the private parts, including chest and buttocks constitutes molestation, even if the kids are wholly unaware that they're both committing serious felonies. Both kids risk being jailed for long periods of time and then branded sexual predators, ruining their lives forever, all for being a normal adolescent. Romeo and Juliet would both be jailed today for their crimes and branded sexual predators, regardless of what their families thought. John Smith is a sexual predator under our legal system for having taken Pocahontas at such a young age. As would be many Popes, and who knows how many dignitaries from days of yore.

Such indiscretions are no longer tolerated in our legal system, even if the two decide to stay together, marry and raise a family.

I'm heavily skeptical of a society wherein the laws permit the heavy handed prosecution and incident persecution of the unsuspecting elderly and innocent minded children.

Be aware that crime no longer requires criminal intent, nor any harm to occur. All you have to do is commit a potential crime, or a non-consentable crime, and all your dishes are done.

This has to change before we ruin too many more families.

Ch. 4. Mandatory Minimums Can Ruin Anyone's Life

"25 years! But she doesn't even have any parking tickets."
"Doesn't matter. It's a mandatory minimum even for first-time offenders. If she walks into court and throws herself at the mercy of the judge without negotiating a deal with the prosecutor beforehand they will absolutely give her 25 years in prison" I was explaining to the now distraught young father.
"She's not even 25 years old!"
"Well unfortunately. The bottle of pills that your daughter took from the pharmacy is a schedule 1 narcotic the intended sale of which carries a mandatory minimum of 25 year sentence. At this point we're going to have to persuade the prosecutor to change the charges. That's the only way we can get her anything near a just sentence, but I think they'll like her because she's generally a good girl: goes to school, has a job, and has never caused any trouble before."

Mandatory minimums are now replete in our justice system. They tie judge's hands and put judicial power into the hands of the executive prosecutors. As a Defendant, in many cases you're at their mercy.

If you use a gun in any crime in Florida, you face ten years just for having the gun, twenty years if the gun is fired, and life in prison if anyone is injured in the act. This may seem like just tough sentencing in a world where gun violence seems prevalent, but consider the dilemma you'd be in if you were innocent.

Americans naïvely assume that should they be so unfortunate as to enter the criminal justice system, that their friends and neighbors who constitute that system, are bound by our merciful cultural traditions to treat them decently. While this is generally true, in regards to their actual treatment, the implementation of today's current public-policy procedure to the first time suspect is often shocking.

The punishment that potentially accompanies most crimes is so shockingly severe that most defendants end up taking a plea deal from the state's attorney rather than having their day in court and potentially facing a life altering sentence.

That effectively robs people of a complete defense. **You don't get your day in court, because you're not willing to risk it.** The offer is often one tenth of the potential punishment, so most prudent people will take that deal rather than rely on their attorney, the Judge, the system, the prosecutor, and the jury to all play fair in the system.

As a criminal defense attorney I spent the first half hour of just about every interview that I ever had – and we're talking about thousands – attempting to reassure my new clients that they were, in fact, still inside the United States of America, and that they were still, in fact, guaranteed the rights outlined in the Constitution, irrespective of how they had been treated by law-enforcement personnel who arrested them, and regardless of the conditions under which they were possibly held for a period of time. This was always an uphill slog.

In the end, sometimes they got justice, and sometimes not, and it always seemed capricious as to who got what.

From facing twenty-five years in prison at the outset, and with the prosecutor's acquiescence, I was able to get this young lady a short jail sentence which she was able to serve most of working as a cashier at a local sandwich shop near the courthouse. I'm sure she's back on her feet now after a hefty scare given her by the justice system we have in Florida.

Another man was not so lucky. At one point I had the occasion to represent a poor, young, black father recently released from prison for selling crack. His wife, the mother of his two children, remarkably had stayed with him throughout the ordeal. Now the kids were about two and four years of age, though they had spent very little time in those years with their father.

My client's latest trouble was of the same nature as his prior offenses which does not bode well for one's sentencing. Now at first you might question why he was reengaged in the business of selling crack, but let me tell you how this particular incident went down.

My client was minding his own business at home when he received a call. The caller claimed to know my client, and to be desperately in need of some crack. However, the caller was really an undercover police officer perpetrating a sting operation. The caller was adamant about their past relationship and about his sincere desire for drugs, and requested that my client meet him at a nearby convenient store. After some resistance, the details of which came out in the deposition of the officer, my client agreed to meet the undercover officer at the location that the officer designated. When my client arrived, he was jumped by several officers and forcibly searched. Crack was found and my client was arrested.

When I deposed the arresting officer he admitted under oath that he had apprehended my client prior to the actual crime of sale, and that they even searched my client without permission. Normally those two factors, an unconstitutional search and seizure, should work to suppress the evidence which ultimately led to my clients conviction. But no matter how many cop shows you've seen wherein clients get off on a technicality, I can tell you that is exceedingly rare. I was only able to accomplish successful suppression on one occasion, and that was when it became clear that the officer on the stand at the hearing was being deceptive as determined by the judge. Most of the time, unless the need for suppression is clear and compelling, the judge trusts officers to act in good faith and merely reprimands them to be more careful next time, and allows whatever questionable facts there are into evidence. Such was the case with this defendant.

He decided to go to trial and try to expose the officer on the witness stand in the hopes of the jury would sense the inappropriateness of the officers behavior, and give the defendant the benefit of the doubt. When the officer took the stand he testified differently from the way he had in his deposition. On the stand the officer testified that the defendant had given him permission to search him, and that therefore the drugs were found pursuant to a lawful search. Even though I pointed out the discrepancy in the officer's sworn testimony, the jury nevertheless believe the officers new account on the witness stand, and convicted my client.

The total amount of crack involved was one rock, just enough to get high for one night, the cost of which was around $25. For this transgression, and for the audacity of having brought his case through the trial process, my client was given eight years in prison. That was the day I knew I had to get out of criminal defense. I simply cared too much about these people. I wept for the young mother, and for their boys, knowing they would grow up without a father, and also for the young man who would likely lose his family forever. A more complete tragedy could hardly have been scripted for their family.

Is important to note that my client was convicted under a particularly grievous statute, which carried a mandatory minimum prison sentence. The aggravating circumstance of my client's unholy act, was that he was apprehended within 1000 feet of the church. The supposition of the statute is that he was actively involved selling drugs to church parishioners, which was patently ridiculous. My client had gone to the location designated by the officer, and probably didn't even know the church was around the corner. Unfortunately, for my client and anyone selling drugs in my jurisdiction, the fact that he was not engaged in selling to parishioners is never considered, only the distance to the potential marketplace.

In Florida we have a statute which considers it to be an aggravating circumstance to drug sales if a person is caught within 1000 feet of a church, school, or convenience store. If you think about it the one universal quality of convenience stores is that they are convenient. They are commonly within 1000 feet of one another. The public defenders office in my county did a study on the map to try to determine if there were any locations in the city that were not within 1000 feet of a church, school, or convenience store. Not surprisingly it was determined that the entire city was covered by this statute with the exception of a few strips of land.

At one point the judge that I was regularly in front of bravely denied to enforce this statute upon one of my colleague's clients, pointing out the overbroad nature of said statute. The state's attorney appealed the judge's denial, and the appeals court overturned the judge forcing him to impose the sentence pursuant to this burdensome statute. Swing and a miss.

The late Nancy Reagan once infamously said "If you are casual drug user then you are an accomplice to murder," and that's pretty much how everyone still treats drug users, despite the fact that during the last presidential election cycle every one of our presidential candidates admitted to having been a casual drug user in their past. Between one half and two thirds of our federal inmates are in custody for drug charges. Let me say that again so that you know it's not a misprint. One half to two thirds of our federal prisoners are in custody for drug crimes, crimes of inappropriate ingestion. Google it if you don't believe me.

Now realize that all drug crimes are *thought* crimes. The concept is that if you take drugs you will be in such a horrible state of mind that you will go out and commit other crimes. Of course if that were true, you would be subject to prosecution for those other crimes, and there would be no need for you to be prosecuted for your ostensibly horrible state of mind. With a drug crime, you can be convicted of your "horrible" state of mind even if you never commit any other illegal acts. Most mandatory minimum laws stem from drug laws.

One final word on mandatory minimums. They may in fact increase the murder rate of certain victims. Serious criminals usually know the potential punishment they're facing before they undertake their crime. Juvenile rape often carries mandatory minimum sentences which range from decades in prison to life in prison, especially if the victim is under twelve. While that may seem just, when one considers the situation from the standpoint of the perpetrator, things become very dark. If the child lives and testifies, the sentence can be life in prison, but if the perpetrator kills the victim after the rape, then there's one less witness to the crimes, and sometimes that makes all the difference. Thus the sexual predators, unable to control their primal urges, may be influenced to kill their victims, because that caries no further penalty than life, and lessens their overall chances of conviction. Thus such mandatory minimums present an even more heinous ultimate outcome for the victim than rape.

Ch. 5. The Repugnant Become Irrelevant, Ignored, And Indicted

Me: *"The offer is six months jail, and that's a bargain"*
Husband: *"Man, that sucks. I didn't even do anything.*
Me: *"You didn't register in time, and that's all they need. You have to register as a sex offender every time you move within 48 hours or it's a new felony charge, you know that."*
Husband: *"I know."*
Wife: *"This is bullshit. How am I supposed to take care of the bills and the kids while he's in jail."*
Me: *"I know, it's a crappy situation, but that's the law."*

Currently the worst stigma you can have in the USA is to be branded a sex offender, of which there are varying degrees, all of them bad.

I know what you're thinking. "He's a sex offender, he deserves it." But maybe your attitude would change in you knew that the offense for which he's now required to register for was perpetrated on his wife, before they were married, when they were both kids. He was 20, she was 16. Now they have four kids and they're happily married, but the state doesn't see it that way.

According to the state, they had sex when she was too young, unable to consent, despite her family liking the guy, and despite his commitment to her, which was still strong, and despite practically zero danger of him ever repeating his crime.

The law sometimes sets arbitrary age limits on people and reacts sternly when those lines are crossed. Sex offenses are of that nature. No judgment is allowed. It truly wouldn't matter if all parties involved including both families, the judge and the prosecutor we're completely fine with the relationship, the law demands harsh punishment if certain aged people interact in otherwise natural ways with differently aged people.

Recently the Legislature in Florida passed a so called "Romeo and Juliet" statute in recognition that sometimes young lovers exist and that's ok, but it too sets an arbitrary age differential, which if the parties fall outside of, there's no room for anyone to exercise judgment to move the bar.

And Everybody Hates sex offenders, even other inmates. I can guarantee you Jared Fogel will be repeatedly and regularly beaten and almost certainly raped by the other prisoners for being a sex offender in prison. In fact, I just looked it up right now and found this on wikipedia: *"In March 2016, Fogle was assaulted by another inmate, reportedly because the other inmate hates child molesters."*

I once defended a young mother for felony child abuse. The facts of her alleged crime were as follows. She noticed a rash on her female toddler's private parts, so she took her to the doctor. The doctor discovered that child had chlamydia. The woman was given treatment for her child and sent home. The doctor, as every doctor in United States, was under penalty of felony arrest to report any suspicious incidents to law-enforcement which may involve the abuse of a child. Chlamydia is a disease that can spontaneously arise in women, however it's also commonly a sexually transmitted disease. There was a reasonable possibility that someone had sexually abused the child. The mother had a boyfriend with whom the child was sometimes left for short periods of time, but who she, in no way, suspected as an abuser. Over the next couple of days, the mother again left the child with her boyfriend. The doctor's call is a mandatory report to the Department of Children and Families in Florida who must pay every child in every complaint a visit. They arrived at the mother's home and questioned her about the child's contact with other adults. When they heard that a boyfriend had unsupervised access to the child, they concluded not that there was probable cause to believe the boyfriend had abused the child, since there was little evidence that any crime had been committed, much less that it was committed by him, but rather that the mother had committed child abuse for exposing her child to the possibility of abuse by leaving her with the boyfriend, so they simply arrested the mother. They never pursued the suspected actual abuser, but instead slammed the mother with a felony charge for potentially having exposed her child to a potential abuser who was not even a suspect in any investigation. We managed to talk the prosecutor out of a prison sentence for the mom, eventually, but she still has a felony conviction for child abuse on her record, probably for the rest of her life. Was the child actually abused? We may never know. But mom paid the price. And we had to fight DCF tooth and nail for the woman to even keep her child.

As for the rights of even accused sex offenders, most people don't give a damn and never will, so don't let yourself become one of the forsaken.

Ch. 6. Sentences Vary Widely

Training attorney: *"You wanna go to the jail?"*
Me*: "Sure"*
Him*: "C'mon."* He handed me a few files as we walked out the PD's office and headed towards the adjacent jail. *"These guys are yours. See if they want to plea out if they've got enough credit for time already served since they were arrested, and if they do, sign em up."*
Leafing through the files I noticed their time in was all over the range. Some had been in for months, others weeks, others just a few days. Also, the charges were different. Some were for improper driving, some minor theft, some domestic violence.
Me: *"How will I know if they have enough time?"*
Him*: "Well you just kinda look and see."* He took a file and flipped it open. *"See, this guys got 37 days in, he's good. This guy has only 17, so he probably can't plea out yet on this charge. See if he'll take 30 days. Oh, and if*

*they're on parole or probation, don't plea them out until
we can talk to their other attorney."*

I was surprised at the variation in the sentences people
were getting. The difference between 30 days and 60 days
is practically unnoticeable from the perspective of the
criminal justice system. This was rather surprising to me
because that same difference is so huge to the defendant.
How could it be that there was such an incredible
disconnect between what people might suffer for minor
offenses and their perception of the same.

The answer is that the system is really an arcane system
that treats people with broad strokes and doesn't
contemplate too much individuality. As society evolves,
the areas in our culture that attract the most attention get
the most progress, and the ones that people don't want to
think about stagnate, and the criminal justice system is just
about the last thing on anyone's mind, because nobody
cares about criminals anyway.

Our criminal justice system is a relic of the 19th century. It
has a distinctly "Wild West" feel to it. Justice is often
harsh, and somewhat arbitrary. Sentences vary widely from
defendant to defendant. There is a uniform method of
calculating potential sentences, but there is substantial
variation in the charging, and thus the range of the
outcome is huge.

Real crime is one of two distinct kinds: hurting somebody, or damaging someone's property. All other crimes are extrapolations of these two types. I suppose you could even reduce it to one, and say "hurting you," including your stuff. At least that's how it used to be.

But today, crime has been expanded. You're rights as an American used to expand until they come up against another person's rights, but not anymore. Now you can come up against the State, which really means the prosecutor, and while that may sound like any other person, they're a lot less understanding of a perpetrator than the general public, and often far less than even the victims.

The difference in sentencing between whether you fight or not could make the difference between spending years in prison or getting probation.

Ch. 7. Of All The Levels Of Trouble, Most People Can Only Handle Level One

In Florida we have ten distinct levels of crime, but for all practical purposes if you're in trouble, you're basically in one of about three or four levels of trouble. No matter which you're in, assume it's Level 4 from the outset, because things can change in a hurry.

Level 1 - Traffic stops

This is the level we all know about. The standard police encounter out on the beat. This is how most Americans view the system as a whole.

Americans expect to be treated with respect even if they're suspected of having violated this level of offense, because there has to be some warning track, and this is it.

Usually, the maximum fine for such transgressions is a hefty fine. Usually in the hundreds of dollars range, and there could be more than one. These alone could be budget busters for most folks.

This type of police encounter is enough to get your heart going, and test the cool of even confident people who are seasoned communicators, and it can freak out normal people.

Nobody likes to be interrogated.

Level 2 - Misdemeanors

Unfortunately, after level one things take a considerable jump in most jurisdictions. The least severe offense that you can commit in the state of Florida carries a potential maximum penalty of sixty days in jail. Kablam! Two months. If you, like many Americans, live month to month, a two month sentence can be enough to wipe you out financially, get you evicted, get your car repossessed, get you fired, and on the road to divorce.

At Level 2 already the penalty can be a year in jail for misdemeanors. This is for minor offenses, like touching someone without their consent without harm, or driving on a suspended license the first time, shoplifting, or possession of marijuana, or a pipe. For any of these things, you could potentially spend a year of your life in jail to atone for your heinous sins.

Consider a typical Friday night out on the town for any aspiring college student. He or she finds themselves in a car with several people passing around a joint in a state where that's not legal. Suddenly they're pulled over and our subject, along with everyone else, is arrested after the driver mouths off to the police. They're each facing a year in jail, so they'll all take the plea deal, even if the joint never reached them.

Level 3 - Felonies

These are what should constitute serious crimes, and while they sometimes do, at other times they represent crimes you can commit without even trying. Martha Stewart is a convicted felon. Do you really think she knew she was engaged in a criminal undertaking, or that she just got too close to a prosecutor? What kind of nation imprisons Martha Stewart?

For minor felonies penalties range up to five years in prison. In Florida, we have an 80% rule, which means you must serve at least 80% of your sentence, so if you get five years, you're going down for at least four.

Offenses can be added together even if the separately offending acts were done at the same time. For example, if you get some cocaine and smoke some out of a pipe, then get in a car and get pulled over, you face 11 years in prison, five for the coke, plus five for the dirty pipe, plus one for driving under the influence, even though all you were trying to do was have some fun.

And forget about it if you then get into an accident and someone dies - you will not see the light of day for years, even if the accident would have occurred whether you had the cocaine or not.

The severity of crime in the US is measured by results, not intentions. **Accidents are criminal these days if the harm is great enough, regardless of the state of mind of the perpetrator.**

Level 4 - Major Felonies

In Florida, we have life and death sentences for many offenses. If you're in above Level 2, you absolutely have to mortgage the house to get the best attorney you can hire to get you out of as much trouble as possible. The rest of your life depends on it. Our courts hand out twenty-year sentences like Christmas cards.

Ch. 8. Jail Is Just The Beginning. Torture Is Real And Rampant

Whenever I hear of water-boarding as a form of torture I have to chuckle. If you're being water-boarded, all you have to do in that situation is keep in mind they probably won't kill you. So you choke and gag a bit and maybe pass out for a second, no big deal, there's no real pain involved, seriously, unless you're afraid of drowning, then it would be awful, for sure, but that's a small percentage of people.

We've got a Way more tortuous system going on right here in the Land of the Free.

We've got major problems in jail populations, the length of time we jail people for, the conditions under which they serve out their sentences, and finally our expectations of them upon their release.

Let's address these in reverse order.

First, what do we expect of people upon release?

It's a good idea to start here so that we know how to treat whoever it is we want to incarcerate.

Ideally what we want is for every person to emerge from prison and rejoin society as a productive member.

All prudence suggests that may not be remotely possible. Recidivism is incredibly high, on the order of 90%. But we have to believe that if the system were reformed, that number might drop considerably. It might be realistic to shoot for a 50% recidivism rate in the near future after considerable reform, which would at least give us diminishing return customers.

In any event, we should not abandon hope that offenders will ever successfully rejoin society.

The reason we have written laws, is so that our citizens don't get out of hand whenever someone gets out of hand. That is, if someone looses their cool, and commits a crime, the other citizens don't have to form a lynch mob to get justice, they can just call the cops. This serves two purposes. First, it prevents the conflict from escalating into larger family feuds and then regional conflicts and so on. Second, it mitigates the sentencing and puts a level head on the trial and outcome, as opposed to leaving it in the hands of the lynch mob. Victims almost always want harsh revenge. An eye for an eye, or worse. We shouldn't let the aggrieved set the punishment, and we don't.

Still, punishment is harsh, and very little education or rehabilitation assistance is available inside.

The conditions inside US prisons are as follows:

Between half and two-thirds of the inmates in federal prison are in for drug crimes. Forceable rape is widespread, drug use is rampant. Corruption is also prevalent, so you can't even fully trust the guards.

We allow torture. Everything from the simple denial of a blanket or toilet paper, up through allowing inmates to exact punishment upon one another in the form of physical violence, right up to putting people in solitary confinement.

We still have slave labor in the USA still. It's in prisons, where we have millions of prisoners who can be made to work for pennies on the dollar, and certain groups and corporations benefit fiducially from that arrangement.

The Torture of Solitary

There is a place in every prison that scares all the inmates. It's called "the Hole," or "the Boot," or "the Dungeon." Think about that for a minute. There are real dungeons in every prison in America, and it's called solitary confinement. Prisons have figured out what our military has not - that seemingly non-violent torture drives men crazy. Humans are social creatures. Putting men into solitary deprives them of interaction and therefore their whole identity.

We have maximum security prisons in America where people are in solitary for twenty-three hours a day. The reports say that drives them insane. We never hear about it because they're in for life, and we never worry about them rejoining society. Nobody gives a hoot.

Ch. 9. The Recurring Nightmare That Is Probation

If you're not going to jail as punishment, just about the only other option is Probation. Probation means you have someone to report to and to pay. It's kinda stupid, and it's spun out of control at this point.

The concept is not terribly bad. The concept is that rather than jail, the court can order you to do some stuff, and then they need someone to keep track of whether you did it or not, and that's a probation officer. It's an attempt to micromanage people's lives for the better, but just seems to get in the way of their living.

One problem is that it ends up being just a layer of bureaucracy that they pay for who are living off of the convicted. There are drug testers, and class providers, and now an entirely new layer of probation liaisons. All of them exist ostensibly to assist in rehabilitation, but the convicts would all be better off if they were just left alone. Hit them with some initial punishment, then let it go.

There's a saying people have in Florida that illustrates the problem: "Come for vacation, get on probation, return in violation, stay for the duration."

It's a trap. I once had a client request two additional years in prison rather than accept five years on probation.

It perpetuates the cycle of incarceration by leaving you vulnerable to the whims of your probation officer. If they don't like you or they're a jerk, you're in for a hellacious ride.

It's incredibly easy to violate probation, and in Florida, any violation, no matter how slight must be reported and can be grounds for revocation of probation and incarceration. For example, if you've ever been late for anything important, you're at risk.

Another problem is that it turns people into second class citizens. If a person is safe enough to be out of custody, they're safe enough to be left alone.

Ch. 10. You Can Go To Prison For The Rest Of Your Life Having Never Been Convicted Of Any Crime

Whenever I tell people about the law I'm about to tell you about, they don't believe me. I once heard Bill O'Reilly vehemently deny even the possibility that such a law could be in effect in the USA, but you can Google it now and see for yourself, so I'll proceed.

Jimmy Rice, was a little boy who was tragically and horrifically murdered by a sex offender who had recently been released from prison. The outrage in the community was palpable. "Something has to be done!" the call went out, despite the obvious laws that were already broken in the commission of the heinous act.

Whenever any law gets passed with some kid's name in the title you know it's over broad. The law doesn't prevent one of the classical crimes *already* outlawed since antiquity, or it would bear that moniker, so it must reach beyond traditional laws, into the grey area of acceptability. Jimmy Rice is a prime example.

The law that was ultimately passed, now called The Jimmy Rice Law, can be summarized thusly: Whenever any person is associated with sex, should they be in custody for any reason, they can be held indefinitely for rehabilitation, on a two out of three vote by a panel of empowered psychiatrists.

I know it sounds vague. It is. But that's what it says in all practicality.

The "associated with sex" part is defined as having been associated with any charge, whether dropped or not, wherein sex was mentioned. The operative qualifier here is that the charges could have been completely dropped, and still the Jimmy Rice law applies. Can you say "double jeopardy?"

The "in custody" part is the only qualifier here. You can be there for any reason, but you have to be in jail for them to invoke Jimmy Rice, for now.

The empowered psychologists are just that. Right out of some Freudian nightmare, someone to judge your sexuality and the authority to recommend indefinite confinement should they so choose.

The holding indefinitely part is real. There are populated prisons in Florida holding sex offenders "until rehabilitation," and the last time I checked, one of them didn't even have a rehabilitation program.

In other words, you can be incarcerated for the rest of your life by a panel of three shrinks without any trial, no attorney, no constitutional rights, nothing. Oh, sure, you get an attorney that helps you verify that they've complied with the Jimmy Rice statute, which is like saying you get someone to help you verify the blades you're about to be tossed into are sharpened and twirling properly.

The bottom line is you have to fight for justice these days, and the discrepancy in sentencing between those who fight and those who do not is cavernous.

This next part of this book will tell you how to fight for your freedom, your family, and your finances in today's justice system.

PART II: HOW TO DEAL WITH THE JUSTICE SYSTEM

Ch. 11. How To Avoid Arrest

Don't Break The Law

"What's the offer from the state?"
"Three years prison."
"What do you think?"
"Unfortunately, they got you over a barrel. They caught you driving red-handed."
"But I'm a driver. How was I supposed to make a living?"
"I don't know, but you cannot drive anymore."
"But I've never had any accidents, No DUIs."
"Doesn't matter. They caught you driving on a suspended license too many times. At this point I'm just not going to be able to protect you anymore."
"What should I do?"
"Unfortunately, the best thing I can recommend to you is that you take the plea deal."

The surest way to avoid arrest is to avoid breaking the law; however, these days that is much harder than it used to be.

That nice guy spent several years in prison at our expense for harm that was never intended and never occurred. A licensing violation - a crime against the state alone.

Trouble comes looking for people these days.

It has become easier and easier to transgress the law in a very serious way without any intention of hurting anybody, and without any harm ever befalling any victims. Whereas in days past the lack of criminal intent, or a lack of intended victim would immediately exonerate anyone accused, today we punish potential crimes, or "pre-crimes," more than ever before.

Today it's possible to spend years in prison for what might have occurred as a result of an accident that never even happened. One could say that thought crimes are real; however, the situation is worse than that, because there is no need for the crime to have even been conceived. Should a state's attorney deem your actions to be offensive, and by extrapolation offensive to the state, they can pursue you with such vast resources that you have few options but to play their game and ride out the system. It's a daunting position for anyone to be in.

So, never trying to hurt anyone and nobody ever getting hurt is not good enough. These days it's critical that you take the necessary care to avoid the appearance of impropriety, and the mere potentiality of accident, or suffer the consequences of the penalties imposed by powerful authorities.

Because the criminal justice code in every state is now so voluminous that no one other than legal scholars could possibly keep track of all of the potential crimes, and because intent, or mens rea as it was formerly known for centuries in the English Common Law, has been removed as a necessary element of every crime, it is incumbent upon all of us to take additional measures to ensure our security from the state.

Avoid The Police

"Forget it. Let's go someplace else."
"Why? We just got here."
"Yeah, but there's a bunch of cops here."
"Seriously? We're not doing anything wrong."
"100%. I'm leaving."

After making every effort to comply with the laws of your state as you understand them, the best thing that you can do to avoid arrest is to simply avoid the police altogether.

I can pretty much guarantee you that if you are not ever where any police are, that you will never be arrested. Done and done. You may receive an arrest warrant, but that allows you to turn yourself in on your own terms, a much preferable way to enter jail if you have to. Also, arrest warrants can sometimes be revoked if the court that issued it can be assured that you'll appear in court, thus you may never have to go to jail even if a warrant is placed on you, so consult your attorney first.

So, if you know where cops hang out, do not go there.

If you happen to know where the Secret Policeman's Ball is, don't crash it.

Never go to a police station or sheriff's office, if you can avoid it and remain safe.

If a bunch of cops decide to hang out at your favorite coffee shop, find another place to hang out. Yes, seriously. It's not a crime, or discriminatory, to avoid cops while they're on duty. A policeman's job is to arrest people, so you don't want to be around when they're working.

Do Not Approach Cops

"I was just petting the horse. I would never hit a horse."
"Well that's what they arrested you for - Assault on an Equine Officer"

If you ever see a cop anywhere ever, do not approach them. They don't want to talk about their car, their motorcycle, their horse, their gun, or anything at all with You, no matter how friendly they're being with each other. That's because, if you think about it, if you were an attacker, you might try to get as close as possible to them by first appearing friendly, So if you walk up to a cop saying Anything, you're still a potential attacker, and that's how you should expect to be treated.

Just ignore them. Even if they're kicking someone's ass, do not approach. They're allowed to kick ass to a certain extent. Assume everything is under control. If things get really out of hand from your perspective, you can record them from a distance, a long distance, but be prepared to be arrested for interfering with police conduct if you do, and be prepared to say goodbye to your camera forever if you decide to be a vigilante for justice.

Unfortunately, there is no established protocol for how you're supposed to treat the cops. Nowhere does it say "You have to remain 25 feet away," or that "You can't raise your voice to, or record police in public." So the acceptability of behavior becomes one to be determined by the cops right then and there. In other words, if they're willing to do whatever it is you want to record, they're probably willing to take you down too. Sure, you're case may ultimately be dropped. After a bump on the head, a few nights in jail, and a few thousand dollars, they'll be willing to forget the whole thing.

And for Pete's sake, if your friends or God forbid, your spouse is going down, definitely Do Not Engage the cops to try to stop them. He or she will need you on the outside. One of you has to remain cool at all times. You can't help anybody if you're in custody too. And if you have kids that you're responsible for, keep in mind that if you get mixed up in any legal shenanigans for whatever reason, it could cause all sorts of logistical issues. Just saying, y'all who vigilantly defend your partners are cool and all, but there's a time and a place, and that time is tomorrow, and that place is in court.

Don't Call The Cops

Me to my Defendant: *"Who called the cops?"*
Defendant: *"I did."*
Me: *"Why?"*
Defendant: *"There was something going on next-door. It sounded like a fight and it was getting pretty loud, so I thought they could help to calm the situation."*
Me: *"Did they?"*
Defendant: *"Well, yeah, they went next-door, and they ended up taking both of them to jail, and the kids went to DCF, but then they came over here. When I was standing at the door talking to them, my wife and daughter came to the door. The officer saw my daughter, and thought my wife look a bit young to have a daughter that age, so he asked them their ages, and they told him. My wife was is only 19,*

and my daughter is four years old. So the cop did the math and determined that my wife was only 15 when she had our daughter, so he arrested me for raping my wife."

The worst part about the above story was that the arrested father was the breadwinner for the family, so that once he was in jail for allegedly raping his wife, there was nobody left to pay the rent and the other bills, so the mom had to go to a shelter to live, their four year-old daughter went into foster care, and the young girl's mother who was also living in this extended Mexican family, and being supported by the dutiful husband, was forced to return to Mexico.

The state destroyed their entire family because of an arbitrary age rule, and it never would've happened if they hadn't called the cops. The sad fact is that the danger you face from the police has now grown past the point where it can exceed the danger that you face from the criminal element present in society.

Maybe as many as 20% of the people I defended over the years were the actual ones who called the cops, and would never have been arrested if they'd just let it be.

I don't care if you're in a live firefight with the neighbors, you've run out of ammo, and Edna is advancing on your ligustrum hedge, Do Not Call the Cops! Ever!…Ok, wait, that's going to get me in trouble. I have to take that back a little bit. That's a bit of hyperbole.

When I say "Don't Call Cops," please understand that if you feel that you or someone else is in danger, then by all means call for help. What I mean is "Don't Call the Cops for Stupid Reasons." Keep in mind that if you get the police involved, the situation better be very serious, because it's about to get deadly serious now that you've involved armed guards with authorization to shoot to kill if they feel their life or someone else's life is threatened.

So, do not call the cops to get your cat out of a tree, or because your neighbor has a broken tail light on his car. Do not call them over financial disputes, especially if the dispute is with your drug dealer. Do not call them because your child did not clean his or her room, or because you caught your husband or wife with another person, again, unless someone is in actual imminent danger already. There are all sorts of other legal procedures for such occasions, but many people, for some reason, instinctively call 911. Don't do it. Prudently evaluation the situation, preferably after a cooling off period, and if you still feel it necessary to involve the police, then perhaps it's necessary.

So, to review and How to Avoid Arrest:

1. Don't Break the Law
2. Avoid the Police
3. Do not Approach Cops
4. Do not Call the Cops (except in the case of imminent bodily harm)

Ch. 12. How To Deal With Police

Sometimes you really want to go to an event where you know for sure cops are going to be, like a sporting event, or an airport, or an encounter cannot otherwise be avoided. Here's a little advice for those hopefully brief situations.

You're goal is to minimize your exposure to the law enforcement personnel, end the encounter as soon as practicable, and go about your day. To that end, you should always be looking for an exit, and then taking it. Don't be shy about asking if you can leave, and then exiting at the first opportunity. Distance is your friend. You can deal with legal trouble much easier with your lawyer and the judge than you can with the police.

Be aware of their presence in certain environments. You are at your most vulnerable driving on the roads.

If a police officer gets behind you in traffic *without* his lights on, turn off at your next opportunity, preferably towards an innocent location, as fast as possible without arising suspicion. Wait there for a minute, adjust your radio or something, then get back on the road and continue on your journey. If you turn off the road too fast, that in and of itself may cause the cop to follow you, so try to be cool. This is just a little extra protective measure for your most vulnerable situation, driving.

If a police officer gets behind you in traffic with his lights on, pull over at the next safe location where you can both safely get out of your cars without getting hit by other passing vehicles.

It's a good idea to always keep your drivers license, your automobile insurance, and your state automobile registration receipt together *above your head* in the sun visor of your car just in case you do get pulled over. That way all the information that is usually requested of you is right at your fingertips, and in a location that does not force you to make any furtive movements when you go to retrieve same. Reaching your hand into a big purse or underneath the seat to recover your wallet unfortunately exactly resembles the movements that you would take if you were reaching for a weapon. The recent killings of Alton Sterling in Louisiana and Philando Castile in Minnesota unfortunately illustrate this problem perfectly.

The best thing that you can do in any traffic stop situation is to try to reassure the officer, via your smiling, friendly, and polite interaction, that you are no threat to them at all. Tell them who you are in the community: where you live, work, and go to church. Once the officer knows that their safety is in no way jeopardized, your encounter will proceed much more smoothly.

If you do happen to get pulled over, or encounter the police via a walk up, politely offer your assistance immediately. *"Yes sir, how can I be of assistance?"* That lets them know you're on their side.

Hopefully they won't strip search you, or forcefully withdraw your blood, or otherwise handle you roughly, but they can if they want to, they might if you give them an excuse, and they probably will if you give them any good reason.

Most encounters will only last a few minutes unless you're being arrested. You'll be questioned and asked to comply with a few commands and a request or two, like searches.

Obey All Commands

Most assuredly, you'll be commanded to do some things. For example, "Stay in the car." or "Get out of the car." One officer I talked to said no matter which you first choose to do, he would ask you to do the other, just to see whether you would obey his commands, and how.

So, obey all the commands of anyone wearing a badge forthwith. Do it immediately, but not using any sudden, or big, jerky motions.

If you're being ordered to do something you don't understand, or that could be interpreted two different ways, you can ask for clarification of the order.

Again, obey all orders such as "turn around," "get up against the car," "spread your legs," "put your hands behind your back," and "get into the car." None of these things mean you're being arrested. They can do all that for officer safety, or to secure you in a secure location.

At some point instead of an Order they may Ask you a Question. You'll know the difference. One tells you what to do. The other is a request of you, and the distinction is critically important.

A request for permission from you is almost always a request of you to waive one of your constitutional rights.

Requests usually take the form of a pretty assertive statement that is also a question, like: "You want to let us search your car?" or "You wanna empty your pockets for me, please?"

That is the time when you need to very gently assert your rights. The way to do it is not to throw your knowledge of Constitutional Amendments in their face, rather you want to simply ask "Is that a request?"

When it comes to your Constitutional rights, be polite, but uncooperative. Do not confuse this with refusing any cop's orders. Only be uncooperative when it comes to waiving your rights.

A friend was recently pulled over because he had three people in a two seater car. The officer asked him *"May I search your vehicle?"* His response was *"What is the purpose of your request?"* Her response was that *"I always ask if I can search vehicles for drugs."* His response was then *"There are no drugs in this vehicle, so there's no need for you to search it, so is it ok if I say 'no'?"* To which she responded, as she must, *"Yes, it's ok"* to refuse, and then he did.

Sometimes they'll give you a hard time about refusal, so be prepared to stand your ground. They might say something threatening like *"You better let us search your car, because if you don't, and I arrest you, and then I find something. I'm going to make sure the Judge throws the book at you."* Don't cave. Remember this rule: **If they're asking for your permission, they need your permission.** Otherwise they would be whacking you with a stick to get your compliance.

Waiving your rights always puts you in more danger. It lengthens the amount of time you'll be around law enforcement, and it widens the scope of evidence they can use against you in court. If they arrest you before they've established probably cause, there's a decent chance any evidence they recover can be suppressed.

DON'T F#$@! WITH COPS!!

If you do come into contact with law enforcement in the execution of their duty, and they happen to turn their attention towards you in a way that trips your "Spidey-sense," or they ask you any question the answer to which has anything to do with their investigation, here is what you should and shouldn't say.

Do *not* remind them you pay their salary, or that they work for you, or that they're supposed to be public servants and should be doing something more important. Do not try to be antagonistic, or witty, or condescending.

Do not shout at the officer *"I know my constitutional rights!"* or use profanity, or be impolite in any way. However, you also do not want to be cooperative, because that violates your rights, so assert your rights, gently.

Here are some ways people have effectively asserted their constitutional rights in the past:

"Is it ok if I say 'no' to your request until I can talk to my attorney about it?"

"I would love to answer that question for you (or comply with that request), as soon as my attorney gives me permission."

"One of my good friends is a real jerk, and he's also my attorney, and he made me promise that if I were ever asked any questions by any law enforcement that I would immediately call him no matter what time of the night it was and let him counsel me about my situation, so can we call him right now?"

The only thing you're legally obligated to say if you're being investigated by police is your legal name, otherwise you can remain silent.

You must allow yourself to be searched for weapons. This is supposed to be a minimally intrusive "pat down" search, but how you handle it can make a huge difference. If you say *"I don't have a bomb up my butt,"* you can expect a thorough cavity search for said bomb.

Don't be a jerk to the cops. They have sticks and they're allowed to use them. Nobody ever questions a black eye, broken nose, or a bump on the head a defendant gets during arrest. Don't get your face smashed into the concrete for your witty repartee.

You must follow orders to move if your physical presence could be considered trespassing at your current location. You're not entitled to be on private property. There is some leeway for being on public property, but you can't interfere with businesses or the inner workings of the city or you'll be properly taken down.

The key to keep in mind here is officer safety. The officer is allowed to take any reasonable measures to ensure his safety during his investigation. That includes placing people in handcuffs, and into vehicles while being questioned.

What To Do If The Cops Come To Your Residence.

There's a distinctive, authoritative, compelling knock that cops use. You can usually tell it's not your neighbor. Be prepared.

Knock! Knock! Knock! Knock!

"They knocked on my door like that for 30 minutes. They were calling my name, and saying 'We know you're in there. Just come out,' but I just sat in my room. Did I break any laws?"
"No Sir, you did not."
"Then I called you."
"Good move."

There are very few reasons cops knock on your door that are good news for you. If a cop is at your door, it's almost always bad news. Usually, it's because they're looking for someone or something. Those are the two kinds of warrants that are commonly issued: an Arrest Warrant, and a Search Warrant.

A Search Warrant empowers the cops to come inside. If that's what they've got, they're coming in, after they announce themselves, hopefully, though the announcement requirement has largely gone away.

An Arrest Warrant is different. It only entitles them to enter private property if they reasonably believe the person they're looking for is present. There are many clues to someone being present, but clues may not be enough for them to enter **as long as they don't see you.**

There's a rule in American law that operates like a warrant called "The Plain Sight" rule, and it states that if an officer sees something illegal in plain sight that gives them probable cause to act accordingly.

Thus, if an officer looks in your window and sees a pile of cocaine on your table, guess what, they're coming in to get those drugs, and you, and whoever else they see has access to those drugs.

Similarly, if an officer sees you inside your own home, and they have an Arrest Warrant for you, again, they're coming in.

However, if there is no search warrant, and nothing in plain sight, the officers will have a very hard time justifying a forced entry on suspicion that you're inside. Unless of course they can hear you, which corroborates other clues, and gives them permission again.

So, if cops are at your door and you don't want to help the cops, or get arrested, shut up and stay out of sight, that's your right. You can do this no matter how long they bang on the door, and they will for a while.

If you're being arrested - being placed in a car for officer safety is not usually considered arrested - you must comply with orders about where to go and what to do, or your actions will constitute a new crime of resisting arrest which can stand alone by itself even if the underlying charge is ultimately completely dismissed.

I cannot tell you how many people I've defended for the sole charge of Resisting Arrest.

If you're being arrested, **Go Quietly**

For your own benefit, keep your cake-hole shut. Don't talk to anyone, especially the officer, about your case. In fact, once you're arrested, don't talk to the officer at all, except to invoke your rights as previously suggested. Keep in mind the old TV line, *"Every thing you say will be used against you."* Not *can*, but *will be*.

You are never allowed to resist any arrest with violence, even an illegal arrest, so don't fight the cops, it just makes everything worse. Prosecutors and Judges Hate defendants who resist law enforcement forcefully, so you can expect harsh treatment throughout your stay, and in every subsequent police encounter that you ever have for the rest of your life if you resist, so don't f'ing do it. Be cool during your arrest. You'll get your day in court, and it will go Way better if you were cool to the cops during the process.

As I told all of my criminal defense clients, when you're out in the field, the cops have all the power and the authority to use it, so don't give them any excuse or reason to do so. You will have all the time you need to bring any and all complaints you may have about police procedure to a higher authority later, so suppress any inclination that you may feel to express your gripes to the officer arresting you.

I have actually seen Judges go easier on defendants because the arresting officer gave a positive report on the defendant's attitude during arrest. That's who you want to be.

Ch. 13. How And When To Get A Lawyer

"Hello! Bob! Can you hear me?!
"Phil? Is that you?"
"Yeah, look, I'm in a bit of a spot right now. I'm going to need some legal representation pretty much now."
"...Are those choppers I hear in the background?"
"Yeah, hold on."
"...Are you on the run right now??"
"Yeah, I'm in the woods behind my house. They're looking for me. They're gonna find me pretty soon with the dogs."
"Jesus, Phil, you gotta turn yourself in."
"Yeah, I know, but I wanted to call you first."

This story was relayed to me by another attorney as a true story, and he was just they type of guy to have something like that happen to him. He said he panicked on the phone, thinking he would get in trouble if he didn't immediately suggest to the guy to turn himself in, but that's not exactly an ideal situation.

The lesson in this anecdote is **get an attorney on the phone asap.** Before you turn yourself in, do talk to a lawyer. There are so many ways they can help you out it's ridiculous. Any lawyer will talk to you no matter what kind of trouble you're in **if you have money**.

Most private attorneys charge a reasonable amount for a consultation, somewhere between $50 and $100. Anything less than that is a deal, anything more is probably too pricey.

You should get between a half-hour and and an hour of time with an actual attorney for that amount.

Private lawyers typically charge thousands of dollars for each case. If you have multiple charges, it may be more thousands. You should be able to find a good lawyer for minor offenses for under five thousand dollars, and around ten thousand for more serious crimes. If you're facing decades or life in prison, well no amount is too much to pay for your life, but just about every case can be handled for under twenty thousand dollars. If you're paying more than that, you're probably over paying, but again, if your life is at stake, you get the best you can afford. If the guy you want to defend your capital murder case charges fifty grand, and you've got the money, by all means go ahead and pay him and try to rest easy.

The bad news is, if you have no money, you can't just pick up the phone and talk to a lawyer. The good news is, according to The Supreme Court's interpretation of your 6th Amendment right, you're entitled to have a lawyer, even if you can't afford one, so you will get one soon, and presumably you'll have sufficient time with them for adequate representation.

If the court finds you can't afford a lawyer, one will be appointed to you. The Public Defenders are actual, real lawyers just as much as any other criminal defense lawyer, and some of them are among the best lawyers around. Some of them have dedicated their lives to the practice of criminal defense, and rather than answering to the almighty dollar, they simply work for the state.

I recommend to everyone who gets arrested that, if they qualify for representation by the Public Defender, that they at the very least meet the Public Defender and try to talk to them about the case. If the conversation is fruitless and frustrating, then you know how you'll feel about your representation. On the other hand, if you have a meaningful and comprehensive discussion about the case, and they seem to understand your situation, and offer assistance in the furtherance of your desires, then by all means go with the Public Defender.

More good news, especially for people who committed crime in groups, is that oftentimes the Public Defender has a conflict of interest in representing someone, and in those cases there are private lawyers from the community who step in to represent co-defendants. In other words, you get a private attorney, who would have cost you thousands of dollars to represent you for about $40. Can't beat that.

Once you're in custody, getting appointed to the Public Defender if you qualify should be easy. Representatives traverse the jail trying to make sure everyone gets seen asap, but that could be a while, sometimes months.

Sometimes you make it all the way to court without ever seeing an attorney. If that happens, inform the Judge that you don't know who your attorney is, or that you've not had a chance to speak to them and that you can't afford an attorney, and he'll give you some forms to fill out swearing to that, and appoint someone to you right away. Say this and everything in Court If and Only If it's True - DON'T PLAY THE JUDGE

If you can't get to talk to your assigned attorney, or after you do you're left with a sense of hopelessness, then that is the time to cash in some chips and try to get a consultation with some private attorneys.

They should understand your case. That is, they should be talking most of the time, not you. They should know your charges, the facts, the law, and the local courts well enough to tell you what range of trouble you're in, provided most of the facts are known, or at least discernible.

You should be willing to divulge anything to your attorney. I used to tell clients *"Even if you just killed a bunch of people on your way over here, please tell me, so that I can defend you properly"*

It is an absolutely iron-clad truth that you have Attorney-Client privilege in the law, which means that you can tell your attorney anything about your case, with one exception that should be obvious. You can discuss anything *in the past* with your attorney with impunity, but you cannot discuss *future crimes* that you plan to commit without expecting consequences. Your attorney must act to prevent future crimes even if it means breaking the attorney-client privilege. But All past crimes are AOK to discuss with your attorney, and he or she can never tell anyone what you said without your permission.

Your attorney will act on your side. You can trust that. Your attorney, even if they're being paid by the state, has a primary duty to vigilantly defend you, not to seek justice, but to do the best for you. That you can always trust. It's a cornerstone of our system that remains strong today.

That doesn't mean you shouldn't negotiate with them, you should. After you've discussed your case with an attorney, and you're getting a good feeling about one, if you don't go with a Public Defender (which is only a nominal charge of under $100, an incredible bargain that you can't pass up for the money) it's time to broach the subject: *"How much?"*

"Ok. How much is it going to cost me?"
"$10,000."
"10,000?! Damn can't you help me out a little here."
"Ok, how 'bout $5000?"

Dive right in. As soon as you reach that comfort level where you know you can trust this guy with your life, get a number in your head, and just stop them dead in their tracks, and say *"Alright, suppose I decide to go with you, how much is this going to cost me?"* and do it just like my friend did it in the introductory story at the beginning of this chapter. Whatever number he throws out, react with surprise, and say *"What? Wow. That's a lot. Can you help me out with that?"* and that's it, you're done. Whatever they say next, that's your final price. The reason for this is simple, they've got you over a barrel, so don't struggle. Your only recourse is to go find another attorney, who also wants thousands of dollars up front, and they know that, and they also know the incredible emotional hardship you just went through to explain your case or have it explained, and that you want to go home and crawl in bed now. So, unless you're up for a few days of severe emotional roller coaster riding, take the first reasonable deal from the first person you trust. You may not find another that you trust at all. It's a sellers market.

Once you've picked your lawyer, and made your deal, you're done. That's another nice part about having a lawyer. They'll handle everything. They'll charge you for it, but they'll handle it. If they miss anything, you've got a serious problem and consider finding another lawyer, but many are very competent, and that's what you're paying for, ostensibly.

If you're out of custody, and you're wanted by the authorities, try to arrange with the judge or state's attorney via your attorney for favorable bond conditions. If you contact them via your attorney, and tell them that you want to turn yourself in, and also have a bond hearing, at least you've got a chance.

Some charges are so odious, and some people's individual situations are such that you're not going to get a bond, so if you must turn yourself in, make sure you've taken care of at least all of these details:

- Be aware of the actual charges against you - Call the Clerk of Court in whatever county you were arrested in, give them your name, and they'll tell you exactly what you're charged with.
- Bail money and Bondsmen procedures.
- Bills for which you're responsible.
- Children for whom you're responsible, and Pets.
- Contacts you'll need once you're in custody.
- Cash you'll need to stash beforehand for all kinds of things, but especially bail and emergencies.
- Clothing and jewelry - whatever you wear in will stay in if you're lucky.

- Car - what's going to happen to it if something goes wrong, make arrangements to be dropped off.
- Job - Have your shifts covered if possible.
- Medicine - Do you take any? Do you provide any?
- Time served applied to any other charges you're currently facing.
- Warrants in state and out of state.

From my perspective, it's usually much better to be out of jail while you fight your case (unless you somehow know for sure that you're going to have to do some time), and there are many ways to stay out.

First, try to avoid custody by the method detailed above, but if you do get taken to jail, there is one last trick you can try. The bond clerk at the jail can set your bond at zero after which you'd be released. You can ask them to do so if you can reassure them that you're no threat to anyone and that you will appear for court. It's a long shot, but hey, once you're in the system, you take every shot you can get, they're all long shots.

Trust your attorney's assessment of the case. That's what you're paying them for.

Ch. 14. How To Handle Jail

"Oh my God, you got an extra wash cloth! Get rid of it, quick!"

The jail is a rough place. You never know what can get you into trouble there.

In Florida, every jail is run by the sheriff of that county, and each one is different in terms of how they treat you. The bottom line is, pay attention, do as your told, and try not to cause any trouble.

Your rights are largely gone in jail. You can still remain silent, and you definitely should not talk to Anyone in the jail about your case except your lawyer, but your privacy is gone, your property is gone, your free will is gone. You just go along to get along. In Marion County, Florida, the jail windows are all painted over, the books and reading materials are all gone, and visitation is limited to fifteen minutes per week, and that's all perfectly legal.

Your goal is just to keep your head low until you get released, and to get released asap so that you can be out and productive while waiting for your trial. Bond is a right in the USA, but it's still denied regularly at the outset, or set astronomically high. However unconstitutional that is, your recourse is to have a bond hearing to revisit the amount, and a bond hearing is available on an emergency basis, which means within a few days or a week at most if there's some major holiday.

Your first phone call should be to your best friend who is on the outside who is in a position to help you deal with things by making additional calls and arrangements. That way you can get things done via proxy and get a lot more accomplished. They can help you deal with any of the jail preparation ideas outlined in Chapter 13 if you were unable to handle those before you came to jail. For example, they can help you get money to bond out.

If you have enough money yourself, or you can get it from family or friends, do that. A bondsman typically charges 10% of the amount of the bond as a non-refundable payment, so posting the bond yourself can save you hundreds or thousands of dollars.

If you post the bond yourself, you can expect the money to be returned within a month of the last proceeding in your case, like the trial or a plea. The money will be sent to the address given at the time the bond was paid, which is done at the jail. They're pretty good about this.

If you miss a court date, your bond can be forfeited, and it will be for sure if you miss any significant court date. If a bondsman has paid your bond and you miss your court date, they'll come for you like Dog the Bounty hunter, because if they bring you in, they get their money back. If you've given them collateral to pay the bond, you'll forfeit that if you miss court. Also missing court can constitute another charge. So never miss court unless you're planning on Never coming back. But if you do miss court, do come back.

If you have to stay in jail for a while, you can get trustee status, that's good. It may afford you time outside of the jail, and with the more congenial inmates.

If you find yourself being held for a long period of time without seeing a lawyer or a judge, which happens with more frequency than you want to know, you have one recourse, and it's called "Speedy Trial."

Speedy Trial is a rule which say that you must get a trial within six months for most offenses unless you waive that right. I have seen this card played to perfection on several occasions. Here's how it works.

If you're in custody, you'll be asked pretty soon "Do you waive Speedy Trial?" If there is a reasonable fear in your mind that you're going to be left in jail to rot without ever getting a trial until after you've already effectively served your sentence - something that happens far to often - Do Not waive Speedy Trial. They will ask you, they will beg you to waive Speedy Trial. If you don't waive, before too long you'll have to be brought before a judge. If you still don't waive you'll be given a trial. It's a risky proposition, because you could get forced into a trial at which you could get slammed with the maximum penalty if you lose, even though you received scant representation. On the other hand, I've seen cases dismissed because there were too many cases to try before the expiration of each one's Speedy Trial. That's rare, but it does happen, and it's a powerful right that you should be aware of, and know how to avail yourself of.

If you find yourself being held for a long period of time (weeks) without even being charged, you absolutely should get your case dismissed by the judge if they don't file charges within about 43 days from the date of your arrest. That accounts for all their extensions too, so raise holy hell by sending letters to the judge explaining your situation if you're being held for more then 45 days in the USA without charges. Of course, if you're in Guantanamo Bay or some secret CIA prison because you've been charged with terror related activities, then this doesn't apply, all bets are off, you have no rights, bye bye.

Ch. 15. How To Navigate The Courts

Get a lawyer, asafp.

Let them navigate the courts for you. Press them to answer all of your questions about your situation so that you can be fully informed.

Just so that you understand what they will be doing, and on the off chance that you decide for some bad reason not to get a lawyer and to go it alone, I'll tell you now what to expect from and how to navigate through the treacherous waters that comprise the american criminal justice system.

Recognizing that every state has its own, unique criminal justice system, and that the federal government has yet another, separate, overlapping and superseding criminal justice system, it's still possible to talk about the overall "American" system generally as pointed up by the Supreme Court of the United States on general issues.

So, you've been arrested.

If you're in custody, this chapter will be easy for you. Just pay attention to when people say you'll go to court, and someone from the Public Defender's office or your attorney will come visit you, eventually, before your trial. The jail should bring you everywhere you need to go without you having to do anything. Your transportation will be arranged by the authorities coordinating with the court for your convenience. Just don't miss the bus.

If you're out of custody, and you don't have a lawyer, then you have to navigate the courts on your own, so here's what can you expect.

If you're a suspect in a criminal case in the United States, the procedure is generally the same everywhere. You're entitled to a trial, by a jury if you face jail time, and probably a court date or two to handle any procedural rights you might want to invoke. These court dates will likely be spread out over a few months from the date of your arrest. So, generally speaking, court procedure is sectioned off into different stages of preparation and you'll have an opportunity or two to appear before the Judge before the trial and if you have any major complaints about how the preparations for your trial, that is the place to voice your concerns. Of course, if you have a lawyer, you voice your concerns to your lawyer, their boss, or a new lawyer, and not to the Judge.

If you do not have a lawyer, no one will assist you in preparing for the logistics of court appearance, so here's what you need to know.

All the logistics involved with the case will be left up to you, coldly.

You'll be expected to know where the courthouse is, where the proper entrance is, what dress code is required, and a host of other things that probably won't be explained anywhere except here.

DRESS LIKE AN ATTORNEY. Judges don't usually know everybody inside their court room, and they identify attorneys as the ones dressed in suits. Judges treat attorneys with more respect than they do defendants. If you want to be treated with respect, wear your Sunday best.

Arrive An Hour Early

If you're even one minute late to your court appointed time of appearance, everyone will infer it as a sign of disrespect, including the judge. Often you're not even allowed in at that point, but even if you are, you'll likely be placed at the end of the day's procedures. In other words, you go last. There are simply no excuses at all except death in most courtrooms. I have arrived to court one minute late to find the doors locked and the hearing concluded in the other parties favor, and an unsympathetic Judge unwilling to rehear the case.

NOTE: many judges start court early. One particular judge I remember used to like to start 7 AM court regularly at 6:20.

Parking is often a nightmare it courthouses, and if you're not a regular customer, then you may have to drive around for a while. I have arrived to the courthouse thirty minutes early only to find out that a parking space was more than thirty minutes walk to the courtroom. One hour ought to be enough time to find parking, walk to the courthouse, proceed through security, locate your exact hearing room, and reach it. Anything less than that is risky.

Harsh, grade-school treatment is what you can expect if you miss your court call. Often times you have simply missed your court date, and the judge may have actually issued a warrant for your arrest, which you should try to deal with right then and there. They won't take you into custody if you address it immediately.

Be prepare to be there for the rest of the day. Court days are often discombobulated affairs, and although every court day is designated for a particular purpose, it's entirely possible, and usually likely (unless it is your day for trial) that all types of procedures could potentially arise during any given day. The judge may regularly stop ongoing procedures to address whatever issues are arising.

The judge may even step out into another court room to finish off some other procedure, and then come back to your courtroom to deal with you afterwards.

In The Courtroom

I always thought courts would have signs around, or a friendly bailiff to help people understand what's happening. Not a chance. Once you're a suspect, you're a criminal in the eyes of everyone at the courthouse except your attorney and the good judges. Everyone else will treat you like shit. If you stand in the wrong place, or whisper too loudly, they'll shout at you as if you are a child. It's hard to find the person whose job it is to answer even basic questions. Thankfully, in larger courthouses there are help desks.

If you have to get someone's attention inside a court room, because you have some kind of a problem, or because you absolutely must ask question, and you don't have an attorney, your liaison is the court's bailiff. Try to get their attention without standing up, or flailing around. If you can make eye contact with them, you can usually make some type of gesture which will bring them over, and they may entertain very short, very simple questions.

Appropriate questions that you can ask the bailiff include *"Am I in the right court room?" "Has my case been called yet?" "Where is the bathroom?"* And that's about it. Bailiffs are present to protect the judge from you, but the majority of their daily duty is simply to keep order in the court room, keep conversations from getting too loud, or from happening at all depending on the judge's preference, and to throw people out who are under dressed, like wearing a hat, shorts, or something that could be construed as offensive.

The net effect of individually determined, unposted court procedures is that if you don't have an attorney, and sometimes even when you do, you will have no idea exactly when your case will be called. Individual judges are allowed to set their own procedures. Some of them are well-organized, and others suffer from overstuffed caseloads. Some call names off an alphabetical list they leave laying around the courtroom. Others allow a staff member, like the Clerk of Court present, or even the prosecuting attorneys to call the list. Whatever the order, that's the one you'll follow. Go up to the lectern when your name is called, otherwise remain seated. Generally you can sit anywhere in the courtroom, but avoid the front row, which is usually reserved for extra visiting attorneys, or court personnel, and stay behind "the bar" (that little wall in the middle of the courtroom) unless the court's personnel or your attorney motions you up.

Your first day in court will not be any opportunity to talk to anyone about your case. Your first day is reserved for very limited procedures like determining your name, your lawyer, your charges, and your bond.

If you want to talk about your case with someone, talk to your lawyer only. Do not talk to your best friend, because they can be subpoenaed as a witness against you and compelled to testify as to what you told them under penalty of imprisonment. Don't put your friends in that kind of jeopardy.

You can discuss your case with your legally married spouse if you must, but it's generally not a good idea, because they too can be subpoenaed as a witness against you, and compelled to testify not as to what you told them, but as to your actions at any time, which could easily reveal the substance of your alleged crime. In other words, the legal protections for spouses are weak, and you don't want to bring your spouse into the criminal justice system with you.

The best attitude to have about your case is this: Try to go about your normal life as if nothing happened, but take any extra steps you've been contemplating in order to make it better now. Your appearance before the judge will in some ways be a life-competency test. Judges want to hear that you're a productive, integrated member of society, and to the extent that they believe that you are, they're more willing to favorably consider your sentence so that you can go back to being a productive citizen. They don't want to have to worry about you. If they are worried about you, you can expect some forced rehabilitation in the form of extra sentencing.

Here are some specific things that you should do if you're imminently appearing before a Judge.

Pre-Court Preparations

- Get an ID, preferably a DL (driver's license). This gives you an ostensible home, which means you have someplace to go at night and stay out of trouble.
- Get a Job, or further the one you have. Try desperately not to appear before the judge without something to do, even if it's temporary.
- Volunteer - If no one will pay you for work, work without pay. At least you're doing something, and you don't represent idle hands to the judge
- Pay off any child support obligations that might be outstanding, and any outstanding traffic tickets.
- To be safe, do a warrant search for yourself before you go to court. At least then you can't be surprised. If you have an active warrant out for you, if it's from the court you're appearing in, then your appearance there will help, because you're telling the court you're not avoiding the warrant, and that you want to get the case resolved. If the warrant is out of another jurisdiction and it's for anything serious, you can expect to be taken into custody when you appear in court.

Courts in the US do not weigh the facts of a case to determine an ultimate sentence until the proper time, the trial. Until that time, each appearance in court is delineated for a specific purpose. Unfortunately, courts everywhere have different names for the types of court hearings that are scheduled before the trial.

There is always an "Arraignment," which is the appearance where the court determines your identity, whether you want an attorney, and whether you're aware of the charges being brought against you. In some courts this appearance is waiveable if you have an attorney.

There is usually a date called a "Plea date," or "docket call," "general matters," or even "sentencing," or any number of vague, inconsistent terms. This is simply a date for the court to handle normal business, which means accepting plea deals between the state's attorney and defendants, which is how the vast majority of cases get resolved.

Pre-Trial Hearing Conference

Before a trial there may be one formal preparatory hearing, a Pre-Trial Conference, wherein the details of the trial are finalized, and any remaining legal issues are resolved.

If you have any lingering questions about your case, make sure they are all resolved by the end of the Pre-Trial Conference, because after that there may not be enough time to deal with any irregularities or logistical concerns.

Make sure that by now you've identified all potential helpful witnesses to your attorney so that they can be properly subpoenaed. Make sure any test results will be returned before the trial. Make sure all the preparations for your trial, such as the assembly of exonerating evidence including any audio visual displays, have been completed, or will be completed prior to trial.

Plea Bargaining

Unfortunately, you have little choice but to trust your attorney when it comes to evaluating your plea deal.

Your attorney can tell you several things you need to know.

First, they can tell you the maximum penalty you're facing. You can sometimes evaluate the plea offer relative to that maximum. Generally speaking, if the plea deal is far from the maximum, it looks like a good deal. If the plea deal is near the maximum, which is rare except in cases where the statute commands mandatory minimums, then it looks bad.

Second, they can tell you what people who have records like yours typically get in cases like the one you're charged in. You have a "score" in Florida which is comprised of your permanent record plus the new charges. You need to know what that score is in order to effectively evaluate the offer; however, the score can be adjusted substantially by convincing the prosecutor to change the charges against you. That is routine and sometimes necessary to get a just sentence (see the story at the beginning of Chapter 4).

Third, they can tell you about the Judge you're facing and how that Judge typically sentences charges like the one you're charged with. I've been in front of judges on both sides of this spectrum: one didn't accept plea offers from the prosecution, and the other didn't accept plea offers from the defense.

Fourth, they can tell you about the prosecutor, whether they are reasonable, and what kinds of mitigating circumstances they consider, if any.

If you have no attorney you get none of that beneficial information.

Ultimately, the decision as to whether or not to accept a plea is yours and yours alone. You take the risk, or do the time.

One final thing you should know about plea bargaining in Florida, which may be applicable in your state, is that if you don't like the State's offer, you can plea directly to the judge. This is Very risky as they can simply give you the max, send you on your way, and it's all perfectly legal. On the other hand, I've been able to use this on several occasions where I knew the judge was more reasonable than the State's attorney to get my client a lesser sentence. If you have no attorney and you don't know the judge, be Very wary of using this method. It should only be a last resort.

Chances are you'll have to make a final decision about whether or not to accept the plea deal by the end of the Pre-Trial Hearing Conference. Most judges try to push people to plea well before trial so that court personnel doesn't have to prepare a jury and go through all the other preparations for trial only to have everyone plea out at the last minute. So, be ready to stand or fold by the PTHC.

Trial

I am not going to discuss the in's and out's of trial procedure here, because if you've reached the trial point, I cannot recommend strongly enough that you get an attorney. Even if you hate attorneys. Even if you believe that your attorney is biased because he is being paid by the same state that pays the state's attorney, take one. You cannot imagine and I cannot express the difference in treatment that your case will receive if you have an attorney. The best way I can put it is like this. Imagine you're in a foreign land and you don't speak the language, and all the people in that land hate outsiders, of which you are one. They have zero inclination to help you, and if you can't understand the language, tuff shit.

If you try to do a trial on your own prepare to be steam rolled by all other participants, and prepare to endure the maximum possible sentence.

Here is what you need to know even if you do have an attorney.

Your trial will be short and sweet, like on the order of a day, or a few days at most, unless you're involved in some incredibly complex white collar murder crime or you're famous, like OJ. Most trials are over the same day they start. It simply doesn't take long to pick a jury and present facts.

Be prepared for the prosecutor to present the facts and you in the worst light possible, and understand that is their right. Your lawyers job is not to prevent them from bringing their side of the story so much as it is to bring your side of the story in a more convincing fashion.

YOU MUST HAVE A PLAUSIBLE ALTERNATIVE EXPLANATION AS TO HOW THE ADMISSIBLE FACTS OCCURRED THAT IS CONSISTENT WITH YOUR INNOCENCE TO WIN.

I know you're supposed to get the benefit of the doubt in a case, but that's not how it works in reality. In real life, you usually must have a more convincing explanation of how things occurred or you will almost always lose. You usually have to present clear and convincing evidence that someone else did the crime, or that no crime ever happened in order to win.

If your lawyer can't articulate to you a plausible alternative theory, you better get another lawyer or be ready to take the plea.

Sentencing

Sentencing is usually short and bitter. Usually the judge agrees with the prosecutor's recommendation and sentences accordingly; however, you are usually entitled to a pre-sentencing hearing on all issues which may make a difference in your sentencing. This hearing is broad evidentially speaking, and many things not allowed in a trial are allowed here. If you can offer any evidence which might mitigate your sentence, this is the last opportunity to present it to the court. Take the swing.

Once you're sentenced, it's all over but the crying. All you can do at that point is ride it out.

Hopefully you'll get probation or a deferred sentence, or at least if you have to go to a jail or prison hopefully you'll get one with books or some kind of educational access with which you can enrich your life for when you get out, if you're getting out.

If you're in, use your time wisely. Establish a routine. Work on the core aspects of your life every day: health, education, socialization. This is a rare time in your life when you don't have to worry about most of the concerns that we have on the outside: rent, financials, maintenance, so you've got time to focus on and help yourself. Do that.

There is a minuscule hope that you might maintain that whatever law you were convicted under gets reformed to the extent that they release you, but our laws typically don't reform retroactively, yet, so even if the act for which you were convicted is made legal, your conviction usually stands anyway, because your crime was *against the state at the time* you did the act, and is thus not forgivable.

So, the best thing to do is to help change the laws now before you or someone in your family is under the ire of the state and it's too late.

PART III: ELEVEN MEASURES TO REFORM THE CRIMINAL JUSTICE SYSTEM

What kind of criminal justice system imprisons Martha Stewart?

Ch. 16. Constitutionalize The Common Law Standard For Crimes: No Actless, Intentless, Nor Victimless Crimes

Even though our system is stratified into two different layers, federal and state, both can be amended by a singular method, amending the Constitution.

During the centuries of development of the English Common Law system which undergirds our own justice system, learned men of wisdom subtly adjusted mens' rights against one another into a masterful mosaic of law that was distilled into a completely practical code of common law. The code recognized that there were certain necessary core elements that should be present in any act that could be called a crime.

First, there was required to be an Act, or in Latin "Actus Rea," of some kind. One has never been able to be charged with a crime under English Common Law for Not Acting. No affirmative action has every been required. Lately in America there has arisen the concept that an "omission" can constitute an act. Failure to register a change of address, for example, can constitute a felony criminal act for certain previous offenders. Now the failure to register yourself for the Affordable Care Act can constitute an act which draws a financial penalty.

We are fast moving into a legal environment wherein acts will be required of you, and if you don't do them, you'll be branded a criminal. For example, if you don't register your kids for school, you can go to jail.

The problems with requiring acts to remain in compliance with the law are many, but the most obvious problem is that what is good for some people may not be good for others, and our legal system was built on the concept that reasonable people can disagree. Now that is changing.

With administrative law, government agencies are allowed to make "reasonable" rules with the force of law which you cannot ignore. If the Department of Health passes an ordinance requiring everyone to exercise every day, and to keep track of same, and report it, then that's what we'd all have to do. It's clear to me, as it should be to you, that the government should never be able to force us, under penalty of imprisonment, to act, even for our own benefit. Otherwise, we may all end up exercising daily, owning a pet, and going to church.

Second, there was for centuries a requirement that the person doing the acting manifest a required malevolent state of mind. There were for some time only eleven crimes, and they all required one to have *intended* to do them. These days most crimes have been grouped under something called "general intent," which is a clever way of transferring intent to do something harmless over into the intent to do something deadly. For example, DUI-manslaughter is a "general intent" crime, meaning that if you generally intended to drive, then you legally intended to commit murder, which is obviously ridiculous.

The reason some kind of mal-intent was required is that there has to be something to reform. If a person acted innocently, they cannot change that behavior into anything more positive, so any rehabilitative punishment is redundant and futile. A state of mind, or Mens Rea, of deliberate intent should be a requirement to incarcerate people.

A third former requirement for some intentional act to be considered a crime was the presence of some contemplated victim. Note that the victim need not be harmed. The thief caught steeling is still guilty even if the shop owner suffers no loss. However, there must be someone who would have been harmed had the act been completed as intended.

Your rights as an American formerly expanded at least until they came up against someone else's rights. This is not the case anymore. Now you can be guilty of a violation against the state. They deem that you would have committed some crime in the future. For example, all licensing violations. You're not condemned for the harm you caused, but that which you might have caused. You're deemed to be culpably negligent even when no negligence has occurred due to your not having a license to act in the way that you did.

The English Common Law standard of crime should be restored so that all three requirements are necessary for conviction of any crime. There should need to be an Act, plus Intent, plus a specifically identifiable Victim for any conviction to stand.

The reestablishment of such requirements would operate to eliminate whole categories of crimes that we have today, specifically drug crimes, driving crimes, and licensing crimes. The elimination of those categories of crime would be of great benefit to society on many levels.

Ch. 17. End The Drug Wars

This measure would have the broadest impact on making things right. We could clear out our prisons, and add productive, non-violent laborers back into the society, and relieve pressure on our overworked, over committed police force. Fully two-thirds of our federal prisoners are in for drug crimes, and about a quarter of our state inmates.

Half of the states have now decriminalized Marijuana. Entrepreneurs are finding opportunities, and states and municipalities are finding tax revenues.

What is needed is clearance from the Federal government, which would allow banks to seek insurance on deposits associated with the new medicine. Until then marijuana industrialists must keep money in large sums of cash to pay their taxes, creating a dangerous lure for robbers.

All persons convicted under what would now be defunct drug prevention statues should be fully pardoned, and their rights fully restored, as Justin Trudeaux has just announced for Canada.

The vast majority of organized crime would be economically undermined if the USA unilaterally recognized ingestion as a personal Tenth Amendment right.

All the murderous strife along the Mexican border is caused by the drug wars, and could be ended almost overnight by legalizing drugs in America.

The USA spends tens of billions of dollars annually to fight ingestions choices to prevent ostensibly dangerous states of mind.

The Drug war has been responsible for the greatest separation between citizens and law enforcement in the last forty years, and has placed more officer lives at risk than any other operation since Prohibition. We ask our officers to do too much by having them police ingestion.

Ch. 18. End The War On Driving

This may be imminent anyway as more and more cars drive themselves, but it remains to be seen how much control will remain with the riders, until then recognize that every driver is afraid of death.

Every time anyone gets behind the wheel of a car they know instinctively that if they steer wrong, the chances of them dying are real. Everyone should know that in every car accident, there is at least one person, the driver, and thus they're the most statistically likely to die in an accident. Even an intoxicated driver knows their in danger and adjusts his driving accordingly. Most accidents are just that, accidents.

All driving crimes could be eliminated without any significant harm to society. In fact, all traffic laws could be reduced to suggestions and we'd be far better off. Every four way stop could be reduced to a two-way yield. One way streets should be eliminated. People know well how to drive safely on roads with oncoming traffic.

As it stands now, the roads are the most dangerous place for you to be, not only due to the dangers of huge hunks of metal careening around, but also because you're a sitting duck out on the road when it comes to being picked off by law enforcement. If they want you, they've got you. Your only shield is the crowd.

Self driving cars should completely change the paradigm of traffic law enforcement. Many people will tell their cars to obey the traffic laws, especially if they're breaking other laws. One rule I heard in jail about how not to get caught was "Break one law at a time."

Statistically speaking, the worst drivers are not the intoxicated, they're the agitated. Next are the speedy, then the sleepy, then the intoxicated. Needless to say, mad and sleepy drivers aren't punished nearly to the extent as the intoxicated even though they're much more dangerous.

End this insanity.

Ch. 19. Licensing Crimes Should Be Eliminated

Licensing crimes, if you think about it, are pre-crimes. You don't get punished for doing harm, you're punished for not gathering evidence in the form of the license that you supposedly have some qualifications to act in a way that should not cause harm.

Licensing has a chicken-and-egg problem. The people who give out licenses do not have licenses to give out licenses. At the top or beginning of every licensing pyramid is some person who could not possibly have gotten a license from anyone. At the head of every licensing scheme is some person who just inherently judges competence and makes up rules about who gets licenses. Oh sure, they follow some procedure, a procedure that they just made up. How can any license be valid? It cannot be.

The system is supposed to raise the professional standards of the licensed, and thus improve their service to their customers. Such protection does not work well. There is little correlation between the test for licenses and proficiency. This is illustrated by the simple fact that licenses are required for professions such as palm reading, and fortune telling, the competency of which can hardly be evaluated.

Just about every accident on the road is caused by someone with a license.

The unfortunate reality is that we have to wait for a harmful act to occur before we act to punish someone for a crime. If that were not the best method, then the most prudent thing we could do to prevent crime would be to lock everyone inside their houses unless they had to take some cleared, permissible action, which I hope everyone can clearly see would be overbroad.

American jurisprudence recognizes that laws can be overbroad, which means they prevent normal actions that reasonable people would take in an effort to curtail more harmful acts in an unreasonable way. We could, for example pass a law that limits the speed limit to 10mph and the result would be a massive saving of lives, and an incredible economic collapse as productivity plummeted, so we don't.

Licensing in all its forms should be made unconstitutional as an overbroad, pre-crime, protectionist paradigm, and outlawed forever.

The result of this would be a grand shift towards congeniality in the police, a clearing out of about 15% of our jails, and a restoration of freedom of movement that would produce a massive uptick in productivity.

Considering that every driver, intoxicated or not, knows in any accident they face death, accidents would number about the same.

Ch. 20. Focus The Prosecutorial Paradigm On Justice

One interesting fact I will tell you is that people know intuitively if they did something morally wrong and if they did, they have no problem atoning for it. But, if they didn't intend to do anything bad, but they're still punished, they're resentful because they know they're being punished for nothing.

This reality combined with the implications of enforcing crimes without criminal intent - such as those associated with driving and drugs - creates a dangerous situation for our police. Real criminals are often repentant when caught. False criminals are resentful and belligerent. Stop a man from stealing from a store and they'll give up and go quietly most of the time. Stop a man from smoking a joint or driving too fast, and they're just pissed off.

People always ask me "How do you deal with all those criminals?" But the criminals aren't the ones who are hard to deal with. The criminals are just like you and me, but having lost their shit for a little bit. For me, by far the hardest group to deal with was the prosecutors. They always seemed to have a very strict view of what is acceptable behavior and never had much sympathy for suspects. I suppose it's difficult to maintain a prosecutorial state of mind and an open mind at the same time. I met very few who could do that effectively, and they were mostly former defense attorneys.

There seems to be an inexorable drive to convict in most prosecutor's minds, and that's their job. I would suggest that we could alter that job slightly and perhaps produce a fairer system. The British system from which ours is largely derived has evolved the charge of the prosecutors a bit producing a more just system in this regard. The singular change is that the prosecutor is required to present what he or she feels is the best case for the accused, as well as the worst. This would seem to be a good way to modulate the singular state of mind towards conviction that they seem to grow into over time.

Ch. 21. Reform Sentencing

There are a host of measures that could be introduced under this rubric that could have a profound impact. Here are a few.

Introduce A New, Lowest Level Crime

This measure is necessary to begin to bridge the divide between the public's expectations and the reality of the harshness of the criminal justice system. In Florida it could take the form of a Third Degree Misdemeanor, or 3MM. The maximum penalty for said crime would be a week in jail, with the average being a day, night, or weekend. The maximum fine would be about $200.

I would then advocate for moving every crime down a notch (made less severe) on the scale. Thus in Florida, everything that is a 1MM, would become a 2MM, and all 2MM's would become 3MM's, 3rd Degree Felonies would become 1MM's, 2F's would become 3F's, and 1F's would become 2F's. In my world, we would eliminate the Death Penalty, and probably Life Felonies as well, and the top level would be 1F's, with an established a maximum penalty of around 15 years.

Fifteen years is a long time. It's long enough for people's entire life to change. After fifteen years, any bad environmental influences they had are long gone. All the people they know may be gone. Their families have even moved on. Fifteen years is long enough for many people to die in prison. If a person survives fifteen years in prison, I feel like God must want them to survive, and they should probably be forgiven after that and given another chance at life.

Eliminate The Death Penalty

This should be done for a host of reasons.

Aside from the impracticability of this sentence being imposed, such as the massive expense, there are good philosophical reasons this penalty should be abandoned.

First, because we still don't know what death is exactly, or exactly what it does to the person who dies. It might send them directly to Heaven or Hell. It might send them nowhere. It might send them back again. It might bring unimaginable pain, or it might not hurt at all. It might be a swift, easy punishment to endure, and may even provide some relief, or some type of feeling enhancement, or even power. That's far too much uncertainty in a punishment for me.

Another reason for the elimination of the death penalty is the elimination of the accused due process rights. All possibility of appeal is extinguished in death. All possibility of exoneration via future technology, or via a reduction in sentencing is eliminated. It allows for no room for error. It goes too far beyond our poor power to judge. There has to be some accounting for mistakes in an institution that can level death, yet the death penalty contemplates no possibility of rehabilitation.

Facing death or life in prison, there is no institutionalized interest in behaving, or of even being human.

Never again should an innocent man be executed by the State.

Eliminate Mandatory Minimums

The entire concept of mandatory minimums is anathema to the separation of powers. The legislature should not be allowed to provide the executive prosecutors with a set of tools that allows them to effectively circumvent the judiciary. The current legal system does that and therefore cannot stand.

Ch. 22. Reform The Purpose And Procedure Of Incarceration

Our criminal justice system has multiple purposes. In Florida, punishment is the primary purpose, then prevention, then rehabilitation. That order should be reversed.

Rehabilitation should be the number one priority of the system, because if we can prevent recidivism, we can eliminate a huge portion of crimes.

Prevention is obviously critical, but beyond incarceration and the threat of further incarceration, there is little the system can do to prevent crime. People and culture prevent crime. Punishment is integral as a deterrent, but the punishments given out for crimes are far in excess of what is necessary to deter crime. Most people don't anticipate nearly the level of incarceration that awaits them should they find themselves transgressing the law, so the punishment has little deterrent effect. People should only be incarcerated long enough to protect the victim and other potential victims, but not longer.

Education should be rampant in jails and prisons. It should be impossible for defendants to get away from education in custody. They should have access to computers and a limited Google, wikipedia, and a host of other educational tools. Online classes should be available for them to learn professions and earn degrees.

Work should be available at reasonable pay. Care could be taken to prevent them from committing crimes from jail, but the emphasis should be on access and training, because that's what they'll need to reintegrate when they get out.

Inmates and those under supervision should be incentivized to do good by allowing them to work towards a reduced sentence. Time could be gained by work, good behavior, and educational achievements. This would help to establish in them the habits they'll need to survive outside the criminal justice system.

Eliminate Solitary Confinement

The entire concept of solitary confinement should be abandoned as unconstitutional cruel and unusual punishment under the 8th Amendment, and torture under the UN treaty. Engendering mental instability is wrong.

Ch 23. Make Legal Forgiveness And Full Restoration Of Rights Upon Release The Default Outcome

Forgiveness is a Christian value but it's also very useful in the legal system.

At the end of their sentences, people's rights should be restored in full. We don't want to maintain another class of citizens who have limited rights. Punishment only ends in forgiveness. Perhaps the victims will never forgive, but our society should.

Today if you're convicted of a felony crime in the US, you lose your voting rights, your right to bear arms, the right to live in available places, the right to work at many jobs, sometimes the right to not have to register with a sheriff every time you move, and the right to be left alone.

All of those rights and any others that are currently abridged upon release should be fully restored upon release.

This gives people hope. It makes for good inmates. And it further takes into account the possibility of mistakes in the system.

Further, we should reform our code such that whenever any act which is considered criminal is made legal, all persons suffering under conviction for that act should be automatically exonerated.

Loosen Gun Laws

I advocate for looser gun law restrictions. Criminals hate it when victims have guns. The number one deterrent that inmates report is their victim having a gun. They don't like the possibility of armed resistance and getting shot any more than you or I do. There is most likely a strong correlation between the perception of the relative arm strength of the general public and a low crime rate. It's possible that thousands or even tens of thousands of crimes are aborted each year due to the perception or knowledge of the criminal of the presence of a gun at the victim's house. Advertising a "Gun Free Zone" is literally telling criminals they'll face no armed opposition in that area until police arrive. I realize some people are concerned that "trigger happy" people cause gun violence, but in reality it takes a special kind of criminal to purposefully pull a gun on someone, and it's rare. We only have one homicide per year for every 36,000 guns in America, which demonstrates our general restraint in the use of firearms.

Ch. 24. Put Live Streaming Cameras And Microphones In Jails, And On The Bodies And Vehicles Of All Law Enforcement Not Engaged In Covert Operations

Body cameras should be mandatory on police and everyone authorized to use deadly force who is not involved in a covert operation, and they should stream directly to the internet and be monitored by an internet watchdog group.

Dash cams and rear bumper cams should be on every police cruiser and they should function automatically upon activation of the police lights and/or siren, and they should record uninterrupted for the next hour, or they should just be left on permanently, and again stream directly to the internet and be monitored by some watchdog group.

Cameras should be everywhere law enforcement operates, which is usually also in high crime areas, and we'd be much more secure. Every criminal knows that cameras may be everywhere and that alone is a deterrent, but nothing beats having a crime actually on camera for assessing guilt or innocence.

Microphones are incredibly useful too, and now technologically easy to deploy. Microphones can do very useful things, like triangulate gunshots, and identify suspects by their voice. They too should be replete where law enforcement operates.

While it's important to note that audio video recordings never tell the whole story, they can provide key evidence that can be effectively evaluated by the trier of fact. Further, the knowledge of their very presence should work to discourage acts which people do not want the public to know about.

These technologies are simply too easy not to use everyday and everywhere in the world of law enforcement.

Ch. 25. Establish And Publish A Protocol For The Public To Safely Observe Police Procedure

One night when I was in law school in Miami I went down to Coconut Grove. The enterprise and entertainment section of the Grove is essentially a convergence of three streets. Restaurants, bars, and merchant shops surround a brick laid cul-de-sac where people hang out.

On this particular night I was simply walking with a stream of people minding my own business when the crowd moved backwards around me to reveal a police officer swinging his baton wildly at anyone near him. As I backpedaled to get away I tripped over a rock which saved me from hit by the swing, and I realized the officer was simply establishing a perimeter by swinging his baton at the crowd. There were several officers outside of a cruiser and they had just taken someone into custody. The officers must have felt threatened by the crowd and just decided to get some breathing room by swinging at people. Everyone moved back and the arrest concluded and they drove away. Of course several innocent bystanders including me were nearly hospitalized from injuries sustained in the establishment of the perimeter.

The above story simply illustrates the problem that there are no established police protocols for dealing with the public. The general public has no idea what their rights are when they're encountering the arrest of another person.

Often Americans want to watch the arrest to make sure that the suspect is not being mistreated. Of course people standing around staring at the police can make them uncomfortable. There's always the question of what the people would do if they determined that the treatment of the suspect was unacceptable.

In order to alleviate all this tension, a protocol should be established for police encounters and published so that people know it the same way they know Miranda Rights.

The protocol should establish acceptable behavior for citizens, such as setting a minimum distance people should maintain from any police action. It should establish acceptable uses of recording devices. And it should inform the public that they are not to interfere with police on the street, and establish a known watchdog group or superior ranked officer or department to notify if they have a problem with police procedure, like a website or an 800 number.

Without an established, published police observation protocol, arrests will continue to be dangerous environments for both public and police.

Ch. 26. Expand Access To The Legal Profession

One of the take aways from this book should be that you should never approach a legal problem without a lawyer, preferably a local attorney who specializes in the field wherein your problem lies.

Smart, educated, confident defendants will occasionally tell me. "I can handle this myself. I'm very intelligent." to which I respond that it's akin to going into surgery without a doctor. You'll most likely die on the table.

Get a lawyer. I know they're mostly jerks, and they're just looking at you as a dollar value, but still, you need one if you're in legal trouble in the USA.

The problem with lawyers is that their profession is extremely well protected, and thus they can charge astronomical prices. Sometime in the not too distant future all licensing should be abolished and you should be able to hire anyone you want to represent you whether they have a law degree or not. This would substantially drop the price and open up the markets to competition creating easier access to competent representation, which everyone needs when facing the full power of the State.

Ch. 27. Conclusion In 5 Points

If you take away nothing else from this book, make it these five points.

1. Avoid cops.
2. Shut up.
3. Refuse the search, Gently.
4. Get a lawyer, asafp.
5. Help me change the system before you get dragged into it and it's too late.

Appendix 1

Protester's Guide

If you plan on going out protesting, here are a few things you should know.

First, if you're black, go back and read "The Talk" again in Chapter 2, and take that to heart. If you're not black you should go read it too because you may be about to get a taste of what it feels like to be black in the USA.

Protesters are squarely in the sights of the over militarized police. While this focus could be changed at the local level to demilitarize low income neighborhoods, it's necessary for large scale urban protest scenarios.

Heavy handed is the required police response to protesters because protests can escalate out of control and mobs can form and create real havoc and do real damage. Criminal elements take advantage of the ensuing chaos associated with mass protests to commit crimes with less chance of getting caught because all the cops are occupied with the protesters at the protest. So the authorities can't tolerate much in the way of mass protests.

From a practical perspective that intolerance manifests as enforcement of private property rights for businesses proximate to the protest. You are not allowed to violate private property rights even to peacefully protest. Nor are you allowed to occupy so called "public" lands beyond the parameters established by whatever authority figure oversees that particular area. That means that you can ultimately be moved around from pretty much anywhere, so don't expect to be allowed to stay in one spot.

You are allowed to carry signs, unless they are deemed offensive. Deeming is done by the local police until you get in front of a judge, but by then you've probably spent a night in jail, so try not to be offensive. Clever beats offensive every time.

You are allowed to yell anything that doesn't constitute nuisance or incite a riot. That keeps you from getting too loud, and from suggesting to a crowd that they behave illegally. When one is addressing a crowd, care must be taken even when employing humor. Local law enforcement may not be fully aware of the nuances of the law concerning jokes, and if they decide you've crossed the line into the grey area where you might be suggesting something untoward, they might take you down hard right then and there and let you fight it out with the judge tomorrow, after you stop bleeding and wake up.

The bottom line is that protesting is not a family affair. It can be dangerous, and it can turn ugly. I'm not trying to discourage anyone from protesting. I'm suggesting that you be smart and effective with your protesting, as opposed to just annoying, obnoxious, or offensive.

The purpose of protesting is to promote change. The method is to draw attention to a message, but there are multitudinous ways to spread a message around these days that don't involve showing up somewhere in person carrying a sign. If you're protesting online, you can't get shot.

Appendix 2

DUI

The general rule about DUI's is they're nasty, you don't want any part of them, so don't do it at all. That is to say, if you have even one drink, no matter who you are, you are presumably over some limit and you should not be behind the wheel. You shouldn't even sit in the car with the keys, because in many states that constitutes "actual physical control" of the vehicle which is the same as DUI, and it doesn't matter how inhospitable the weather is.

DUI is a particularly nasty crime for a variety of reasons: it's expensive, cumbersome, sticky, dangerous, and the effects are lasting, and those are just the legal effects.

The best thing that I can tell potential DUI candidates is to remember your 4th, 5th, and 6th Amendment rights. The 4th Amendment protects against unreasonable searches and requires a warrant for most searches. That means if they're asking your permission, they need your permission, and you can deny your permission. The best way to do that is to invoke your 6th Amendment right to an attorney. You can do this by simply responding to any question by asking the officers *"Is it ok if I speak to my lawyer about answering that question before I answer it?"* Make sure more than one officer hears you ask that question if you're going to use it. Then invoke your 5th Amendment right, which I'm sure you know by now is your right to remain silent, and remember, as I repeat this for the third time in this short book: Everything you say and do will be used to increase your sentence, so don't say or do anything you're not ordered to do after you're arrested until you talk to your attorney.

Curtis Elmore graduated with a Juris Doctorate from the University of Miami, FL; worked for the Public Defender in four Florida counties; appeared as a private lawyer in every corner of the state; spent six months hour-for-hour in jails visiting thousands of clients all around the state; defended multitudinous parents against DCF; opened a private practice against non-paying insurance companies; and later defended hundreds of homeowners in the fray of the foreclosure debacle.

Curtis has trial experience in both criminal and civil law with many victories in both.

Other Books by Curtis Elmore, JD:

Freepublic: The Demise Of Military Governments And Rise Of Volunteerism.

NOTES